AF602078

31 Prayers for My Soulmate

Prayers for My Future Husband.
Seeking My Boaz

DENISE GILMORE

ADISAN Publishing AB

Dedication

To my love, my eternal soul mate and lifelong friend. We shared such intimate moments. I'm grateful for your presence in my life, though you are in another world. Your calm and gentle aura, your image, I have imprinted forever in memory.

Table of Contents

Introduction

Are you longing to be in a romantic relationship that results in marriage? Are you asking yourself, where is my soulmate? Where is the man who will be my companion in life?

This prayer devotional will lead you into deeper relationship with God as you share your longings and desires with Him. It will guide you to rest securely in your Savior as you wait patiently for His timing. You will grow in your character as a woman who finds her wholeness by falling madly in love with God. Your life will begin to produce spiritual fruit as an outpouring of your closeness with Jesus.

God wants to transform your heart by establishing persevering contentment and overflowing joy. This devotional is an opportunity to let Him lead you in fervent prayer for the man, He has designed uniquely for you.

Be encouraged and full of hope as you begin this journey of prayer. God knows your longing for a marriage relationship, and He desires to bless you with an abundant life.

SECTION 1:

Praying for A Soulmate

DAY 1

Longing

All my longings lie open before you, Lord;
my sighing is not hidden from you.

Psalm 38:9 NIV

Hope deferred makes the heart sick,
but a longing fulfilled is a tree of life.

Proverbs 13:12 NIV

Reflection

Have I told God of my longing for a husband?

Prayer

Oh God, you know the depths of my heart. You know my desire for a husband. I have been longing for a husband who will love and cherish me. I do not want to live life single, I desire to be in a relationship. This longing is coming from the depths of my soul as I am searching for the man you have designed for me. Where is he now? Will you show him to me? I long to be in love, to be married and to have children. I lay down my desires before you God and I trust that you will answer me. Build in me hope for my future and even now prepare me to meet my husband. I long to be a woman who is filled with your love so that I can love a husband well. My heart aches in my searching. Please fill my heart with your love and help me to know I am your beloved daughter. As I wait, please give me hope in my longing and please direct my path toward the man you have prepared for me. Amen.

Blessing

May your longing be fulfilled by God.

Your Prayer requests

Prayers Answered

DAY 2

Contentment

Nevertheless, each person should live as a believer in whatever situation the Lord has assigned to them, just as God has called them. This is the rule I lay down in all the churches.

1 Corinthians 7:17 NIV

I know what it is to be in need, and I know what it is to have plenty. I have learned the secret of being content in any and every situation, whether well fed or hungry, whether living in plenty or in want.

Philippians 4:12 NIV

Reflection

Am I living contently and joyfully where God has placed me?

Prayer

Lord Jesus, you have given me new life and bright future through your gift of Salvation. I do not understand why I am without a husband, but I know that you have placed me in this circumstance for a purpose. I ask your provision of strength and courage as I choose to life live filled with joy. Build in me contentment and a spirit of gratitude for the blessings you have given me. Thank you for all the ways you are providing for me. Teach me to be content in singleness and show me how to embrace this season of my life with joy that displays your glory. Please shield me from a grumbling and complaining spirit. Please protect me from envy as I watch others who are happily married. Remind me that your love is steadfast and that you care for me, reassure me that you have heard my longing to be married. Teach me wait patiently for your plan. Amen.

Blessing

May you be content in your current circumstance.

Your Prayer requests

Prayers Answered

DAY 3

Asking God to Provide Husband

Therefore I tell you, whatever you ask for in prayer, believe that you have received it, and it will be yours.

MARK 11:24 NIV

Do not be anxious about anything, but in every situation, by prayer and petition, with thanksgiving, present your requests to God.

PHILIPPIANS 4:6 NIV

REFLECTION

Do I believe God will answer me?

PRAYER

Father God, I have shared my longing for a husband, you know my desire to be married and to have children. I am anxious for this to happen. Thank you for all that you have done for me. Thank you for your blessings and provisions. You are a great and mighty God and I know that you care for me. I ask that you bless me with a relationship that leads to marriage. I ask that you present to me a man who loves you and serves you, a man who has a noble character reflecting your goodness and love. Please provide me a husband who desires to lead me and our family in righteousness. I desire to be with a husband who will be my partner in life, a man who will be a life- long companion and friend. I trust you and I know you hear me. You have promised to answer your children when they pray, if it is your will that I marry, please answer me with a husband. Lord, continue to grow in my heart a persevering faith and unbreakable trust in your ability to provide a husband for me. Amen.

BLESSING

May you cease feeling anxious and in thanksgiving ask God.

Your Prayer requests

Prayers Answered

Waiting

The Lord is good to those whose hope is in him,
to the one who seeks him;

Lamentations 3:25 NIV

Wait for the Lord;
be strong and take heart and wait for the Lord.

Psalm 27:14 NIV

Reflection

Am I trying to find a husband in my own strength or am I waiting on God?

Prayer

Oh God, it is difficult to wait. My heart grows weary of searching and I am impatient in my waiting. Show me how to seek you in this season of my life. I want to hear you and know you deeply. Please build in me a desire to be madly in love with you. My strength will be found in you and I want my hope to be secure in you. I will wait as you prepare me and as you provide a husband. It is you who will orchestrate my future marriage. I trust that you are designing my children. I know you desire to bless me, as you know the longings of my heart. Please hold me gently as I expect your answers. Please prepare my husband and reveal him to me in your perfect timing. You are steadfast and good; your ways are higher than my ways. Please grant me perseverance and develop me into the woman you designed me to be. Make clear your purpose and plan for my life so that I am ready to meet my husband when it is time. Amen.

Blessing

May you wait patiently on God's timing.

Your Prayer requests

Prayers Answered

DAY 5

Asking God to Prepare You

For I know the plans I have for you," declares the Lord,
"plans to prosper you and not to harm you,
plans to give you hope and a future.

Jeremiah 29:11 NIV

For it is written: "Be holy, because I am holy."

1 Peter 1:16 NIV

Reflection

Do I hope for the plans God has for me? How can I prepare?

Prayer

Lord Jesus, you have changed my life. I remember when I did not know you and I went my own way. I made decisions selfishly and did not consider anyone but myself. Thank you for saving me from my sin and selfishness. I ask that you continue to sanctify me and make me holy. Teach me how to love and serve you with humility and grace. Thank you for having plans for me, plans to prosper me, plans that bring me hope. My future is secure with you and I know that your plans include my future husband. Please cultivate in me a desire to know you deeply. I ask that you build my character to reflect your love. Show me how to live with integrity and bless me with spiritual fruit that will encourage others. Make me holy as you are holy for the purpose of your glory. Please prepare me to be a wife who seeks your kingdom first. Build in me a desire to grow in knowledge and wisdom through your word and a ignite a desire within me to cultivate a prayerful life. Amen.

Blessing

May you prepare your heart with holiness.

Your Prayer requests

Prayers Answered

Section 2

The Desires of your Heart

DAY 6

Love and Romance

My beloved is mine and I am his;
he browses among the lilies.

Song of Solomon 2:16 NIV

Reflection

Who will be my beloved? How do I prepare my heart?

Prayer

Dear Jesus, who do you have prepared for me? Who will be my beloved? My heart's desire is to be married, to find love that will last a lifetime. Where is the man that I will love dearly? I desire to be cherished by someone to be called their beloved. Thank you, Jesus for loving me unconditionally. Thank you for calling me your beloved child. I ask that you reassure me deep in my soul of my status as your beloved. Please remind me that you are mine. Your constant affection will generate wholeness in my life. Even as I anticipate marriage, I pray that my focus will always be falling more and more in love with you. You know my heart's desire for love and romance, for marriage. I ask that you answer my prayer in the graciousness of your love. You bring me love and joy as you constantly provide for all my needs. You are a generous God, and I am trusting you to bring a husband that knows you and desires to be in a marriage filled with love and affection. As he searches for me, please direct his path, and bring us together in your perfect timing. Amen.

Blessing

May you find your beloved.

Your Prayer requests

Prayers Answered

DAY 7

Life-Long Companionship

The Lord God said, "It is not good for the man to be alone.
I will make a helper suitable for him."

GENESIS 2:18 NIV

Though one may be overpowered, two can defend themselves.
A cord of three strands is not quickly broken.

ECCLESIASTES 4:12 NIV

As iron sharpens iron, so one person sharpens another.

PSALM 27:17 NIV

REFLECTION

How can my heart be ready to be someone's helper?

PRAYER

Father God, you have designed man and woman to be joined. In the same way, you have designed a husband for me. Please prepare me to be suitable for him. Grow my desire to reflect your love and please shower me with your blessings as I worship you in all areas of my life. I know that you have designed people for community, and I desire that connectedness in a romantic relationship. Please focus me as I place you at the center of my life as well as my future marriage. I will be one strand and my husband the other, you will be the center strand holding us together. Make us iron that sharpens iron as we devote our lives to following you. Please teach me how to be a lifelong companion, helper, and friend, a woman suitable for marriage. Please overwhelm my future husbands desire to know you and worship you, making us likeminded in pursuit of a marriage grounded in your truth. Amen

BLESSING

May your character become suitable for marriage.

Your Prayer requests

Prayers Answered

DAY 8

Sexual Intimacy

No temptation has overtaken you except what is common to mankind. And God is faithful; he will not let you be tempted beyond what you can bear. But when you are tempted, he will also provide a way out so that you can endure it.

1 Corinthians 10:13 NIV

Do you not know that your bodies are temples of the Holy Spirit, who is in you, whom you have received from God? You are not your own;

1 Corinthians 6:19 NIV

Reflection

How can I remain sexually pure while I am waiting?

Prayer

Lord Jesus, you know the struggles that I face as a single woman pursuing holiness. The desires of my body often overwhelm me. I am tempted to pursue a sexually promiscuous lifestyle as I date and search for a husband. I know that you are faithful and that you will give me strength to endure this time of sexual loneliness. Please give me courage and strength as I devote myself to worshipping you with my whole being. I ask that you answer my prayer for a husband, so I have an appropriate way to express my sexual desires. I am no longer my own, you bought me with a price, and I desire to glorify you with my body. I pray that you would help me to remain pure, holy, and righteous regarding my sexuality. Amen.

Blessing

May your body be a holy temple, wholly consumed with the worship of Christ.

Your Prayer requests

Prayers Answered

Children

Children are a heritage from the Lord,
offspring a reward from him.

Psalm 127:3 NIV

"Ask and it will be given to you; seek and you will find;
knock and the door will be opened to you.

Matthew 7:7 NIV

Reflection

When will I have children? How can I become a good mother now?

Prayer

Holy God, you have created the whole world; only you know the plans you have set in motion. I greatly desire to have children. You have said in your word that children are a great reward from you. You have also said that if I ask it will be given and if I seek, I will find. I pray for the blessing of children. Please bring me many children who desire to know and glorify you. I pray that I would become a woman who knows how to reflect your love, comfort, and wisdom so that I can raise my children in the knowledge of you. Comfort me and guide me, as I seek a husband who will join me in my desire to have children. Please show me where to find him. Jesus, you have said that if I knock you will answer. Please answer me out of your overwhelming generosity and abounding love. Please bless me with children who are a bountiful heritage from you, given to me to steward for your kingdom. Amen.

Blessing

May you believe that God will answer you when you knock.

Your Prayer requests

Prayers Answered

DAY 10

Above All Desire God

But seek first his kingdom and his righteousness, and all these things will be given to you as well.

MATTHEW 6:33 NIV

Take delight in the Lord, and he will give you the desires of your heart. Commit your way to the Lord; trust in him and he will do this: He will make your righteous reward shine like the dawn, your vindication like the noonday sun. Be still before the Lord and wait patiently for him;

PSALM 37:4-7 NIV

REFLECTION

Do I delight in God? Am I seeking the kingdom of God?

PRAYER

Oh Jesus, I want to seek your kingdom and your righteousness. I want to delight in you. You know the desires of my heart for a husband and children. Lord, help me surrender control and commit my whole being to you. I trust that you will answer my prayers for my life. Please make my righteousness shine like the dawn and vindicate me openly. Teach me how to wait patiently before you. Show me how to be still, with listening ears as I wait for your will in my life. Please protect me from going my own way. I lay my life down before you, knowing that you are in control of all things. I pray for your blessing and mercy on me as I search for a husband. Give me a spirit that delights in you, Jesus straighten my path I follow you with my life growing in desire for you. Amen

BLESSING

May you find the desires of your heart as you know God.

Your Prayer requests

Prayers Answered

Section 3

Growing Godly Character

DAY 11

Tree Planted by Water

Blessed is the one who does not walk in step with the wicked or stand in the way that sinners take or sit in the company of mockers, but whose delight is in the law of the Lord, and who meditates on his law day and night. That person is like a tree planted by streams of water, which yields its fruit in season and whose leaf does not wither— whatever they do prospers.

Psalm 1:1-3 NIV

Reflection

Am I deeply rooted in Christ?

Prayer

Jesus, I pray I would become like a tree planted by the streams of your living water. Grow my roots, send them down deep, making me sturdy in your truth. I pray that you give me desire to mediate on your word day and night. I desire to be a tree filled with good fruit and leaves that do not wither. Please bless me for my righteousness before you. I desire to walk with you in righteousness and holiness, I do not desire to sit with the wicked and spend my time mocking others. You bring prosperity to those who delight in you and blessing for those who follow you. I desire to be a woman who knows you and believes your truth. I pray that you would help me flourish with your living water transforming me into a woman who is confident and secure in your love. Thank you for your grace and truth, thank you for showering me with love and affection. You have designed me to worship you and I desire to be a woman who knows you deeply and worships you openly. Amen.

Blessing

May you prosper by being rooted in truth.

Your Prayer requests

Prayers Answered

DAY 12

Wisdom

Walk with the wise and become wise,
for a companion of fools suffers harm.

Proverbs 13:30 NIV

She is clothed with strength and dignity;
she can laugh at the days to come.
She speaks with wisdom,
and faithful instruction is on her tongue.

Proverbs 31:25-26 NIV

Reflection

How can I grow in wisdom?

Prayer

Father God, please bless me with wisdom that comes from above. Help me to walk alongside older women who have grown in your wisdom so that I can also become wise. Cloth me with strength and dignity. Help me to know that you oversee my future protecting me from being overcome with anxiety. Teach me to laugh at my own worry and instead turn my face to trust you. Let wisdom come from my lips and let faithful instruction come from my mouth. Season my words with your grace and fill me with your wisdom. Guard me from becoming friends with those who are foolish, those who do not seek your wisdom. I pray that you would prepare me to be a wife that is filled with kindness and truth. God, fill my heart with a desire to know more and more about your character and grow me into a woman who walks with you daily. Establish my life on your truth and help me to rest in your grace. Amen.

Blessing

May you be filled with the wisdom of God

Your Prayer requests

Prayers Answered

DAY 13

Woman of Noble Character

A wife of noble character who can find?
She is worth far more than rubies.
Her husband has full confidence in her
and lacks nothing of value.
She brings him good, not harm,
all the days of her life.

Proverbs 31:10-12 NIV

Reflection

How do I become noble in character?

Prayer

Lord Jesus, thank you for being the lord of my life. I know as I follow you, I will grow in character. Your character is filled with mercy and grace as you pour out love on everyone. I desire to be a woman who pours grace and love out upon everyone I meet. I know that you have designed a husband for me, and I pray that he is searching for a woman who has noble character. Please build my character so that my worth will be abounding in your goodness. I pray that I would be a wife that desires goodness and happiness for my husband so that he can have full confidence in me. I do not want him to lack joy and blessing but abound in love that flows from you. I ask that you continue to mold me into a godly woman, a woman whose worth is defined by my identity as a follower of Christ. Bless me with the gifts that come from your spirit full of purpose for encouraging and edifying those around me. I ask confidently for faith, hope and love as I become more like you. Please direct my path and transform me into a woman of noble character. Amen.

Blessing

May your character reflect Christ.

Your Prayer requests

Prayers Answered

DAY 14

Obedience to God

Jesus replied, "Anyone who loves me will obey my teaching. My Father will love them, and we will come to them and make our home with them. Anyone who does not love me will not obey my teaching. These words you hear are not my own; they belong to the Father who sent me.

John 14:23-24 NIV

But grow in the grace and knowledge of our Lord and Savior Jesus Christ. To him be glory both now and forever! Amen.

2 Peter 3:18 NIV

Reflection

Do I desire to follow the teaching of Christ and obey him?

Prayer

Jesus, thank you for providing a way to be with God the Father through your redeeming love. You have reconciled humanity with God through your death and resurrection. Your word says that those who love you, will obey you. Those that love you belong to you and they belong to your Father. I fervently pray that you would grow my love for you. I ask that my heart would be overcome with love and joy for you as my Savior King. Please cultivate a love in me for your word and a desire to obey your teachings. Please mold and develop me into a woman who lives in the grace and knowledge of you. Thank you for promising to make your home in me as I submit my life to obeying your teachings. I want to be consumed by you and your great love. Please protect me from having a spirit of rebellion against you and grow in me a spirit of submission to your authority. Amen.

Blessing

May you find complete joy in obedience to Christ.

Your Prayer requests

Prayers Answered

Respectful Toward Leadership

Have confidence in your leaders and submit to their authority, because they keep watch over you as those who must give an account. Do this so that their work will be a joy, not a burden, for that would be of no benefit to you.

Hebrews 13:17 NIV

Reflection

Am I respectful towards authority in my life?

Prayer

Father God, you have put different authorities over my life. There are authorities in my family, my community, my church. I pray that you would cultivate in me a desire to be respectful to those who have authority over me. Please give me a gracious and humble spirit, one that is teachable and filled with wisdom. I ask that you continue to grow in me a desire to live under the authority of Christ. Please also prepare my husband to live under the authority of Christ. Please give my future husband a spirit of humility and grace. Teach me to be confident in my status as your daughter and aware of my identity in you. I pray that you would grow my spirit to reflect your goodness. Even now, teach me to be in relationships that are mutually respectful to grow in relational experience before I am married. I pray that when I am ready for marriage, I will have developed a spirit that is gracious, humble, and teachable. Please teach me how to be a respectful wife who is overflowing with your love. Amen.

Blessing

May you submit fully to the authority of Christ.

Your Prayer requests

Prayers Answered

Section 4

Cultivating Good Fruit

DAY 16

Fruit of the Spirit

But the fruit of the Spirit is love, joy, peace, forbearance, kindness, goodness, faithfulness, gentleness, and self-control. Against such things there is no law.

Galatians 5:22-23 NIV

Reflection

Are the fruit of the Spirit evident in my life?

Prayer

Holy Spirit, please invade my being with your presence. I desire to have you as my helper in life. Please guide me and direct me in the path that leads to fullness of life in Christ. I want to have the fruit of the Spirit. Please develop in me a disposition that is filled with love and joy. I ask that you teach me to rest in the peace of Christ and teach me to be a peacemaker in times of conflict. Fill me with patience and endow me with kindness. In all things I desire to be faithful with a spirit of gentleness and self-control. These are the qualities that I want to have as a person, wife, and mother. I ask that you grow these good fruits in me. Please prune off the bad fruit that is holding me back from being filled with these good fruits. Help me to see when I am selfish and full of spite or envy and grow in me a spirit of humility. I desire to be a woman who is pure and holy, radiating your love and acceptance everywhere I go. Please fill me with good fruit and with abounding love as you prepare me for marriage. Amen.

Blessing

May you be filled with the Holy Spirit and abounding with good fruit.

Your Prayer requests

Prayers Answered

DAY 17

Bound by Love

Therefore, as God's chosen people, holy and dearly loved, clothe yourselves with compassion, kindness, humility, gentleness, and patience. Bear with each other and forgive one another if any of you has a grievance against someone. Forgive as the Lord forgave you. And over all these virtues put on love, which binds them all together in perfect unity.

Colossians 3:12-14 NIV

Reflection

Am I defined by the love of Christ?

Prayer

Father God, thank you for choosing me. I know I have not chosen you, but you have chosen me, and I am dearly loved by you. I pray that you would clothe me with compassion and kindness. Build in me a gentle nature a personality that is full of humility and kindness. Teach me to be patient and full of forgiveness. Thank you for being forgiving towards me and for loving me always. I pray that I will have your character as I learn to be more like you. Please lavish me with love overflowing so that I can demonstrate your love to others. I pray that I will be a wife who models the virtue of love, binding myself together with my husband in unity. I pray that I would be merciful and forgiving towards him as you have forgiven me greatly. Please mature me into a woman who walks in your love and reflects your glory. Amen.

Blessing

May you be bound in the love of Christ.

Your Prayer requests

Prayers Answered

DAY 18

Living by Faith

For we live by faith, not by sight.

2 Corinthians 5:7 NIV

I have been crucified with Christ and I no longer live,
but Christ lives in me. The life I now live in the body,
I live by faith in the Son of God,
who loved me and gave himself for me.

Galatians 2:20 NIV

Reflection

Am I living in faith?

Prayer

Jesus, thank you for living in me! I no longer live for only my body, but I live eternally because you live in me. I cannot see you or all that you have planned for me, but I have faith that you are in control. You have given me new life and I will be forever grateful. I pray that you would help me to live my whole life by faith trusting you with everything. I know you are who you say you are, and I have faith that you love me and have a plan for me. Please continue to grow this faith within me, increasing it as I wait for you to reveal my husband to me. I know that you desire to bless me as I have shared my longing for a husband with you. Please increase my faith that you will answer my prayer in your timing. In my waiting, I will be empowered by your love. I desire to be a woman and a wife who is filled with faith in your goodness and mercy. Your grace is sufficient for me and you pour out your blessings generously. I will wait in faith. Amen.

Blessing

May you find yourself full of faith.

Your Prayer requests

Prayers Answered

DAY 19

Known for Integrity

Whoever walks in integrity walks securely, but whoever takes crooked paths will be found out.

Proverbs 10:9 NIV

Because of my integrity you uphold me
and set me in your presence forever.

Psalm 41:12 NIV

Reflection

Are my paths leading toward integrity?

Prayer

Father God, all your ways are good, and all your ways are kind. You have blessed me greatly, thank you for your unfailing love. Please convict me of my life, have I taken the paths that lead toward wisdom and integrity? Have I followed you well? I pray that you would build in me confidence in who you created me to be. Teach me to stand boldly in the gifts and talents you have given me. Remind me I am fearfully and wonderfully made, made for a purpose that you have designed for me. I pray that you would help me to stay focused in my pursuit of growth in integrity. Please do not allow anything to distract me from what you have called me to do. Establish my character and develop me to be holy and worthy of honor. I ask that my integrity and character would be apparent to the man I will marry. Please bring me a husband who acknowledges the depth of my character and desires to honor me as an upright, commendable woman of God. Amen.

Blessing

May you live in integrity.

Your Prayer requests

Prayers Answered

DAY 20

Reputation for Holiness

When you heard about Christ and were taught in him in accordance with the truth that is in Jesus. You were taught, with regard to your former way of life, to put off your old self, which is being corrupted by its deceitful desires; to be made new in the attitude of your minds; and to put on the new self, created to be like God in true righteousness and holiness.

EPHESIANS 4:21-24 NIV

REFLECTION

Do I have a reputation for holiness?

PRAYER

Lord Jesus, make me more like you. Please take my old self and transform me into a woman who desires more of you. My former way of life has not served me well, it was corrupted by deceitful desires. I pray that you would build in me new desires that are in accordance with your plan and design. Please transform my attitude to reflect the fruit of your spirit as I chose to follow you more each day. I want to put on my new self, my new being that reflects your true righteousness and holiness. As I wait to become a wife, I ask that you continually renew me in mind, body, and spirit. Grow me into a woman who will be a wife focused on bringing you glory through serving my husband. Protect me from my old selfishness and grow in me a propensity to put the interests of others before myself. You have made me new and I am delighted to be in your presence transformed by your holiness. I pray that you would bless me through marriage and continue to renew me for my entire life. Amen.

BLESSING

May you be made new in Christ Jesus.

Your Prayer requests

Prayers Answered

Section 5

Praying for My Future Husband

DAY 21

Man Who Fears the Lord

Who, then, are those who fear the Lord?
He will instruct them in the ways they should choose.
They will spend their days in prosperity,
and their descendants will inherit the land.
The Lord confides in those who fear him;
he makes his covenant known to them.

Psalm 25:12-14 NIV

Reflection

Will God also prepare my husband?

Prayer

Father God, thank you for working in my life. I pray that you would also work in the life of my future husband. Develop in him a fear of you that leaves him in reverence of you and your glory. Please show him your power and might and humble him to trust you completely. Please instruct him in the way that he should go. I pray that you would bless him with prosperity and prepare him for the blessing of children. Make your covenant of love known to him as he lives in awe of you and your glory. I pray that he would be brought to his knees in praise of you his King. Reveal yourself to him and show him how to live free in your grace and love. Make known to him the inheritance that you have planned for him. I lift him up as he continues to grow and learn who you are and how much you care for him. I pray blessing over him in every area of his life. Prepare him for relationship with me as he knows you deeper and deeper so that we might be joined in a love that is united by your unfailing love. Amen.

Blessing

May you trust God with your future husband.

Your Prayer requests

Prayers Answered

DAY 22

Upright and Righteous

Surely the righteous will never be shaken;
they will be remembered forever.
They will have no fear of bad news;
their hearts are steadfast, trusting in the Lord.
Their hearts are secure, they will have no fear;
in the end they will look in triumph on their foes.
They have freely scattered their gifts to the poor,
their righteousness endures forever;
their horn will be lifted high in honor.

Psalm 112:6-9 NIV

Reflection

Will my husband be righteous?

Prayer

Lord Jesus, I know that you have created a man to be my husband. I know that you desire what is best for me and that will be a man who desires to live his life to glorify you. I pray that my future husband will be made righteous by your grace. I ask that you give him the strength to stand firm in his identity in you and grow in him a steadfast character. Please empower him to trust in you always. Secure his heart and keep him from anxiety and fear. I pray that he is a generous man who cares for the orphans, poor and widows. Pour out blessing on my future husband, showering him with spiritual gifts. Empower him to extend love to everyone he meets. I ask that he would be a man who loves you and wants to serve you with his life. Amen

Blessing

May you trust God to build the righteousness of your future husband.

Your Prayer requests

Prayers Answered

DAY 23

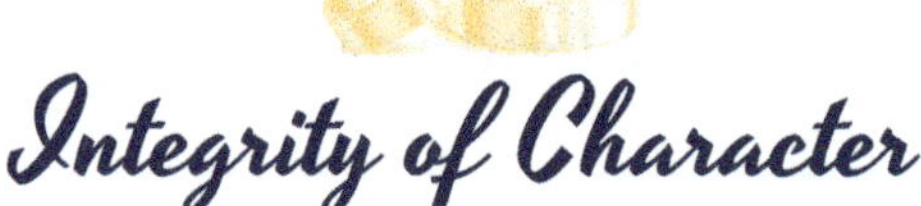

Integrity of Character

For this very reason, make every effort to add to your faith goodness; and to goodness, knowledge; and to knowledge, self-control; and to self-control, perseverance; and to perseverance, godliness; and to godliness, mutual affection; and to mutual affection, love. For if you possess these qualities in increasing measure, they will keep you from being ineffective and unproductive in your knowledge of our Lord Jesus Christ.

2 Peter 1:5-8 NIV

Reflection

Will my husband live with integrity and character based on Christ?

Prayer

Jesus, please add faith to my future husband daily. Fill him with your goodness and instill in him knowledge that comes from you. Build in him a spirit of self-control and perseverance that leads to godliness. Nurture his spiritual growth to include mutual affection for other believers that results in a life that presents evidence of your love. Build these qualities in him increasing the measure of your grace regularly so he is effective in his witness of your gospel. I pray that these character qualities would prepare him to be a husband guided by you and a father full of love and mercy. Please prepare him to lead me and our children in the truth of your word and the steadfastness of your love. Raise him up to be a man of integrity, full of kindness and warmth as he radiates the glow of your affection to those around him. Amen.

Blessing

May you trust that God will grow the integrity and character of your future husband just as he is preparing you.

Your Prayer requests

Prayers Answered

DAY 24

Faithful in Obedience

"If you love me, keep my commands."

John 14:15 NIV

Do not merely listen to the word, and so deceive yourselves.
Do what it says.

James 1:22 NIV

He replied, "Blessed rather are those who
hear the word of God and obey it."

Luke 11:28 NIV

Reflection

Is my future husband living in faithful obedience?

Prayer

Father God, I pray blessing over my future husband as he lives in faithful obedience to you. I ask that he would be immersed in your holy word and learning to life his life to reflect your commands. Please protect him from deception and prompt him toward obedience. You have blessed those who have heard your word and obeyed it. Please bless the man I will marry as he faithfully follows you. I pray that you would increase his love and desire to know you. Give him an enduring love for you as his savior and God. Teach him how to love you with all his heart, soul, mind, and body. Give him ample opportunities to love those around him. Please surround him with your presence, your love, and your affection. Amen.

Blessing

May you trust God to grow the faithfulness of your future husband.

Your Prayer requests

Prayers Answered

DAY 25

Demonstrates Honor to Women

Husbands, in the same way be considerate as you live with your wives, and treat them with respect as the weaker partner and as heirs with you of the gracious gift of life, so that nothing will hinder your prayers.

1 Peter 3:7 NIV

Husbands, love your wives and do not be harsh with them.

Colossians 3:19 NIV

Reflection

Will my future husband be respectful toward women?

Prayer

Lord Jesus, I trust that even now you are preparing my husband for me. I pray that he will be a husband who is considerate of me as we live together. Make him a man who will be gentle with my feelings and respectful of me as a partner. Please teach him that I am also an heir in your kingdom, your child and beloved by you. I pray that he would know the height, depth, and width of your gracious love so that his prayers would be never ceasing before you. I ask that you grow him to be a man who pursues gentleness and humility never dealing harshly with those around him. Teach him how to shower me with your love. Season him with grace and mercy that comes from your kindness and compassion toward him. Amen.

Blessing

May you trust God to bring a husband who will shower you with love and honor.

Your Prayer requests

Prayers Answered

Section 6

Praying for Future In-laws

DAY 26

Blessing on Mother-in-Law

"Haven't you read," he replied, "that at the beginning the Creator 'made them male and female,' and said, 'For this reason a man will leave his father and mother and be united to his wife, and the two will become one flesh'? So they are no longer two, but one flesh. Therefore what God has joined together, let no one separate."

MATTHEW 19:4-6 NIV

REFLECTION

Will my mother-in-law include me?

PRAYER

Holy God, I want to pray a blessing over my future mother-in-law. Please bless her with goodness and bring joy to her life. I pray that you would honor her for her perseverance in raising my husband. I pray that I would be a blessing to her and a welcome member of their family. I pray that we develop a friendship which is mutually affectionate and covered with love. Please help me to respect her and love her for who she is. I ask that you build in me a gracious spirit that is seasoned with humility and compassion for the woman who has borne and sustained my husband for many years. Please bless her and comfort her as she allows him to separate to be united with me in marriage. Show me how to best love and respect her as I learn to love her son. Amen.

BLESSING

May you accept your mother-in-law and appreciate the time and effort it took to raise your future husband.

Your Prayer requests

Prayers Answered

DAY 27

Blessing on Father-in-Law

"Haven't you read," he replied, "that at the beginning the Creator 'made them male and female,' and said, 'For this reason a man will leave his father and mother and be united to his wife, and the two will become one flesh'? So they are no longer two, but one flesh. Therefore what God has joined together, let no one separate."

MATTHEW 19:4-6 NIV

REFLECTION

Will my father-in-law approve of me?

PRAYER

Almighty God, my father-in-law has a special place in my husband's life. He has trained and taught him about life, imparting wisdom, and knowledge about many things. I pray that I will respect my father-in-law and honor him as a leader in my husband's life as well as my own. Shower blessing upon my father-in-law as he allows my husband to become a leader in his own family. I pray that he would be encouraged and affirmed in his character as he watches his son live to glorify you. Please unite my husband to me as we learn to make decisions on our own as a couple. Graciously surround his relationship with his father as his father's leadership becomes wisdom and gentle advice. Teach me how to show respect and love to my father-in-law as I learn to be part of his family. Amen.

BLESSING

May you respect and honor your father-in-law.

Your Prayer requests

Prayers Answered

DAY 28

Blessing on Future Siblings

How good and pleasant it is
when God's people live together in unity!

Psalm 133:1 NIV

Reflection

How will I fit with my future husband's siblings?

Prayer

Oh Lord, I pray a blessing on the relationships with my future husband's siblings. I pray that we would all enjoy one another and love one another as you have loved us. I ask that you grow a culture of unity and peace with us all. Please prepare them for me to join their family. I pray that we would feel as though we have always known one another, comfortable and happy. Build in me a desire to grow in relationship with a whole new family. I pray that these people I have not yet met would know you and grow in relationship with you. Make them strong in character and filled with your spirit. Grow out from them, filling them with good fruit and bless them with spouses and families of their own. Strengthen the whole family in the power of your love. Amen.

Blessing

May you feel secure in Christ's love as you learn to love another family.

Your Prayer requests

Prayers Answered

Section 7

Waiting with Anticipation

DAY 29

Hopeful Anticipation

You are my refuge and my shield;
I have put my hope in your word.

Psalm 119:114 NIV

And hope does not put us to shame, because God's love has been poured out into our hearts through the Holy Spirit, who has been given to us.

Romans 5:5 NIV

Reflection

Do I have hope in God to prepare me a husband?

Prayer

Lord Jesus, you are my hope and my salvation. You are my strength and my courage when my heart grows faint. I put my hope in your word and trust in your promises. I know that you desire to bless me, you hold my hope and you have prepared my future. You laid out good works that you have prepared in advance for me to do. I know my hope for your provision of a husband who knows you and glorifies you with his life will not be put to shame. Your love has been poured out over my heart and the Holy Spirit has been given to me as a helper. I will hide in you and wait for you to bring me a man who is ready to unite in marriage with me for the glory of your name. You know the desires of my heart to be married and have a family. You know I long for a companion, a man to love me and cherish me for this life. I trust that your will for my life is the best plan for me and I will wait with hopeful anticipation for your timing. Amen.

Blessing

May you wait for your husband with hopeful anticipation.

Your Prayer requests

Prayers Answered

DAY 30

Letting Go

"But blessed is the one who trusts in the Lord,
whose confidence is in him.

Jeremiah 17:7 NIV

Humility is the fear of the Lord;
its wages are riches and honor and life.

Proverbs 22:4 NIV

I have been crucified with Christ and I no longer live, but Christ lives in me. The life I now live in the body, I live by faith in the Son of God, who loved me and gave himself for me.

Galatians 2:20 NIV

Reflection

Can I surrender my desire for a husband to God?

Prayer

Father God, thank you for your great love and mercy on me. Thank you for always providing everything I need and for having a plan for my life. In humility I have asked you to bless me with a husband. I desire to be married and I long to have a loving companion. I trust your plan for my life, and I surrender to your will for me. You know my desires. I am no longer my own I am now living for the glory of Christ. Please make it clear to me the direction you want me to go. I lay down my desires for marriage into your hands and I will rely on you for strength as I wait for your answer to me. I have faith that you will sustain me, complete me, and fill my life with enduring love and happiness. You have given your life for me and I desire to worship you in spirit and truth filled with the faith. Amen.

Blessing

May you be confident in God's plan for your life.

Your Prayer requests

Prayers Answered

DAY 31

Expecting Blessing

"His master replied, 'Well done, good and faithful servant! You have been faithful with a few things; I will put you in charge of many things. Come and share your master's happiness!'

Matthew 25:21NIV

And my God will meet all your needs according to the riches of his glory in Christ Jesus.

Philippians 4:19 NIV

Reflection

Do I expect blessing from God?

Prayer

Jesus, you have surpassed my expectations time and again. You have given me life to the fullest and you have taught me how to seek your kingdom first. I am growing in my character and my love for you and others expands every day. I still desire to be married and I know that you will answer me in your timing. You have trusted me to glorify you in small things and now I will wait for you to trust me with the many things that come with marriage. I know and trust that you will continue to meet all my needs according to your glorious riches. You are a great and generous God who desires to lavishly bless your children with goodness and joy. You desire to share your happiness with those who are faithful to you. I trust that you will care for me in all circumstances. I am waiting expectantly for the blessings that you will shower over my life. Amen.

Blessing

May you wait expectantly for the lavish blessings
the Lord will pour out before you.

Your Prayer requests

Prayers Answered

Final Blessing

Every good and perfect gift is from above, coming down from the Father of the heavenly lights, who does not change like shifting shadows.

James 1:17 NIV

May you recognize the gifts God is sending from above. Your Father is the Father of heavenly lights. He has designed the world and is the keeper of time. You are handcrafted by your Maker and your future is secure in His hands. God desires to bless you abundantly and he knows the depths of your soul. He has designed a man specially for you, a soulmate for your mutual enjoyment. Christ will complete your life and work all things for his Glory, in His time. Be patient, pursue Christ, and remain hopefully optimistic. The Kingdom of God is yours to receive. He has entrusted you with the desires in your heart for a purpose and they will find fulfillment. In Jesus Name Amen!

www.ingramcontent.com/pod-product-compliance
Ingram Content Group UK Ltd.
Pitfield, Milton Keynes, MK11 3LW, UK
UKHW020140300726
14059UKWH00007B/4

9 789189 452336